JOANNA YOUNG is an amateur walker and pa...
She works as a civil servant for the Scottish Exec... other
Leith.

Joanna inherited a passion for the Hebrides from her
family. Her maternal grandmother was born on Benbecula,
the daughter of a minister from Shawbost in Lewis, grand-
daughter of the Stornoway postmaster. Joanna's paternal
grandmother Eilidh Watt, born in Skinidin, Glendale, was a
well-known Gaelic writer and broadcaster. Her family were
crofters from Glendale, although Eilidh claimed to be able
to trace her descendants back to the Viking Askill who
founded what was to become the MacAskill stronghold in
Rudh' an Dunain.

Short Walks on Skye

JOANNA YOUNG

Luath Press Limited
EDINBURGH
www.luath.co.uk

First Published 2006

The paper used in this book is recyclable. It is made from
low-chlorine pulps produced in a low-energy, low-emission
manner from renewable forests.

Printed and bound by
Digisource (GB) Ltd., Livingston

Typeset in 10.5pt Sabon

For Robbie, Laura and Jennifer,
without whom this book would not
have been written

A Message from the Publishers

OUR AUTHORS WELCOME feedback from their readers, so please let us have your comments and suggestions.

Whilst we make every effort to ensure that information in our books is correct, we can accept no responsibility for any accident, loss or inconvenience arising.

Contents

Preface

THESE WALKS ARE all exceptionally short. Each can be done in less than 40 minutes one way. Some only take five minutes. But all of them take you to places of wonder and beauty: if the weather is good you may want to stay for hours, if not all day.

The forty walks are spread across Skye, mainly hugging the coastline, with a few on the neighbouring island of Raasay, and one on the mainland. The location of the walks is shown on the map overleaf.

Remember that car journeys on Skye can be surprisingly long, especially if you are travelling on minor roads. You may want to plan your walks around the area in which you are staying, rather than trying to cover all of the island's 'wings'.

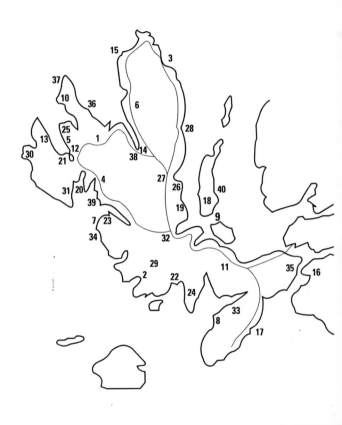

Map of Skye showing location of Walk Routes

Introduction

THIS BOOK DESCRIBES forty short walks on Skye: the shortest is only a couple of minutes, the longest no more than 35. These walks will take you to some of Skye's most magical places: beaches and bays, rivers, woodland walks, churchyards, ruined castles and forts.

There are a couple of mountain walks, but in the main I have exploited the endless opportunities provided by Skye's coastline. I would be struggling to think of anywhere else in Britain that offered such a wealth of short walks to places of such outstanding natural beauty.

The walks begin at the Fairy Bridge: an old bridge in a beautiful setting, strongly associated with Skye's past, both ancient and modern. The book finishes with a description of the walk to Hallaig – the ruined crofting township on the east coast of Raasay made famous by Sorley MacLean's poem of the same name.

The walks fall into four simple categories:

- **Easy Magic:** taking you in 5 minutes or less to some wonderful spots, often far from the madding crowd.

- **Quick History:** short walks of up to 15 minutes that include some historical interest at the end point or en route.

- **Walks on the Wild Side:** an exhilarating series of walks that don't take too long – no more than 25 minutes – but go well off the beaten track.

- **Highways to Heaven:** a series of slightly longer walks, with relatively good and clear paths – but no walk is longer than 35 minutes.

Why short walks?

You do not have to be super fit or have oodles of time to be able to enjoy all that Skye has to offer. You may not be used to walking far or exploring on your own. Don't worry. These short walks will encourage you to get out of your car and see how much of the island can be accessed with relative ease.

You may be travelling with family and friends who have mixed levels of fitness, confidence or motivation. You may well have youngsters with you who react with horror at the very notion of a 'walk'. Never fear. All of these walks are short enough to do with children and most take you to places that they will really enjoy exploring. Some of the very short walks in the first section can be included as 'pit stops' to get everyone out of the car for some fresh air if tensions in the back are mounting.

Despite its image as a land of hikers, Skye lends itself to short walks. It's something to do with the weather. If it is a really beautiful day it will be so hot and so gorgeous that all you will want to do is walk for a short while and collapse on a beach or dip in the river. If it is rainy or showery the prospect of a long soaking is not always that appealing – you are often looking for something that can be fitted in between showers.

You will no doubt stumble across your own short

walks on Skye. Many of the routes here are short versions of longer routes and you could experiment with others. The realisation that I could 'cheat' by taking the first or the last stretch of a longer walk and turning it into a short version was liberating for me. Once you break free of the tyranny of long walking I am sure you will start to find many more possibilities!

You might find other hidden gems by driving along a minor road and exploring once you get to the end of it. You won't always know what you're going to find and it won't always work, but it's definitely worth trying – there seems to be some kind of magic round most of Skye's corners.

A sense of time and place

Walking is the best way of getting a proper sense of place – of height, of distance, of where one range of hills stops and another starts, of the connections between islands and headlands and sea lochs, of the link between one place and another.

It is also a great way of absorbing the history of the island. In part this is just by being there; the sense of history in some spots is quite palpable. The passion for the places makes you want to learn more about what has happened on the land where you are walking, to understand the lives of the people who used to live there. History books come alive when you are familiar with the places they describe. The history and the land feed off each other and bring each other to life.

I have tried to aid this process by including some

short snippets of local information about each walk, and to include a large number of walks that take you to a place of historical interest. In a book of this size, though, what I can convey is necessarily limited. There are many wonderful books on aspects of Skye's history and I have included some suggested further reading at the back.

Food for the soul

Spending time on Skye is good for the spirit. It doesn't work for everyone, and if your first experience is truly blighted by days of torrential rain or swarms of midges you might never come back for more. But most visitors do experience a sense of awe and wonder at being in such a beautiful and thrilling place; for many it is a place to return to many times and refresh the soul.

Three weeks researching this book had the same effect on me as the *Summer in Skye* enjoyed by author Alexander Smith back in the 1860s. Like him I was escaping from the heat of Edinburgh and the drudgery of the year's work gone past: 'Jaded and nervous with eleven months' labour or disappointment, there will a man find the medicine of silence and repose'.

I hope that these short walks will inspire you to get out and about in Skye – to discover its history, to explore its coastline, to admire its jagged mountain peaks, to breathe the soft air, feel the wind in your hair and gentle rain on your face, to find 'the medicine of silence and repose' – in short, to let the island work its magic.

Practicalities

What the descriptions cover

ALL THE WALKS include directions on how to travel by car and where to park. Finding the right starting point is often half the battle, especially with these lovely short walks. The sketch maps also show the routes in and suggested parking places. Please use your own judgement though, and park carefully.

The sketch maps indicate the route to the end point. This should be read with the detailed description of each walk. I have tried to write this in as non-technical a language as I can and also to be realistic about what to expect. I think it is better to know in advance if you're going to end up sinking into bogs or clambering up cliffs, as well as reading up on the wonders that await you at the other end.

Some of the places may look a little different from the descriptions you find here. This is a living island – fences may go up, ruins crumble down, and the coastline itself is always changing given the constant onslaught from the sea. The storm of January 2005 was violent enough to move rocks and boulders and the landscape of some places may have altered again as a result.

Each route has an 'at a glance' description of the path type so you can assess what kind of footwear is required. But I would strongly recommend good walking boots for *all* walks on Skye, however short, to take proper account of the roughness of the terrain and the wetness of the ground.

The most critical part of each description is the answer to the question 'how long will it take?' I have tried to be as accurate as I possibly can here, including information on the difference in time it might take to go up and go down, or where you need to factor in time to pull your feet out of the bog or to re-find a sheep track that keeps disappearing. Remember also that walks take longer on a nice day – you have to keep stopping to admire the view or take photos (and it is amazing how much faster you can walk when it's pouring with rain!)

The time highlighted is the time it will take you to go one way. Unless stated otherwise, double this to work out how long it will take to go there and back. For the few routes that are circular I have quoted the time at the halfway point for comparative purposes.

None of these walks is very far. The longest is 2.3km, and most are under 1km. I have not quoted the precise distances, as they are all so short. In any event it is the *time* not the distance that really matters. Some long walks with a good path take a lot less time than a shorter walk that requires you to go cross-country.

The sketch maps will help you on your way but I would also recommend taking an Ordnance Survey (OS) map with you. You may well want to walk a little way off the beaten track or extend the short walk into something longer.

I hope you find these descriptions and categorisations a useful way of guiding you to the walks that will best suit you and yours.

Skye and its surrounds

Not all of the walks are on Skye. Three are on Raasay, a small island off the east coast of Skye (I apologise in advance for any offence caused when I use 'Skye' as shorthand to cover both islands), and one is on the mainland at Glenelg. The latter is included mainly to encourage people to take the ferry crossing to Skye.

The three Raasay walks are included because they are wonderful walks in their own right – but also as a way of tempting you over to the island. Raasay is well worth a day's visit (although try and find a way of staying longer if you can). If you take the car over it is expensive but does give you the freedom to explore to the north and the east. It would allow you to get to the start point for the walk at Hallaig, for example.

If you go by foot you will save a lot of money but can cover a lot less ground. There are, however, lovely forest walks – too long for this book – leading off from the old railway at the ferry terminal. Walking there is a haven of tranquillity – when I was last there I walked for two and a half hours from the ferry without seeing a soul.

Finally, some practical tips for exploring Skye by car and by foot:

1   Use passing places on single track roads to overtake or let cars by.

2   Watch out for sheep on the roads.

3   Journeys can be unexpectedly lengthy on Skye
    – leave plenty of time, allow extra for bad roads
    and don't be over-ambitious in what you can
    cover.

4   Park carefully – don't block gates, passing places
    or turning areas.

5   Keep dogs on a leash.

6   Close all gates behind you.

7   Respect your environment – take all of your
    rubbish home with you, leave the wildlife to
    itself, and treat ruined buildings with care and
    respect.

8   The weather changes rapidly – be prepared for
    sun, wind and rain – and don't forget about
    the midges.

9   Strong boots are advisable for even the simplest
    of walks – it can be wet and rough underfoot.

10 Don't forget to slow down, look up, breathe in:
    there is no rush on Skye.

PART ONE

Easy Magic:
Five minutes and under

ALL OF THE WALKS in this section take you, in just a few minutes, to places of absolute wonder and beauty – beaches and bays to explore, a river to dip in, or a vantage point over a piece of Skye's history. Some of the walks are so short they can hardly even be described as such. They are included to inspire everybody, whatever their circumstances, to get out of the car and breathe in Skye's magic.

Some of the places are perhaps inevitably well known on the tourist trail – if you can access them easily from a car you can get there from a coach too. But many are further off the beaten track and you may well be able to enjoy your spot of hidden magic in solitude.

None of the walks is more than five minutes long. Some could be extended if you wanted to by walking further once you get to your destination – for example the large beaches at Glenbrittle near the Cuillins, or Eyre Point on Raasay. The time given is the time to get to the end point rather than to explore once you get there. But the places are so beautiful in themselves that it won't feel like a chore to walk further, more like a reward.

The walks include:

Fairy Bridge: A quick scramble around one of the most scenic and magical spots on Skye.

Glenbrittle Beach: Stroll to a wonderful beach in the shadow of the Cuillins.

Beach near Staffin: Two minutes' walk to a gorgeous hidden beach.

St John's Chapel, Caroy: Leafy churchyard at the head of a sea loch.

Dunvegan Castle Jetty: Panoramic views of the castle and sea loch.

Hinnisdal River: Quick scramble to a river swimming pool and picnic spot.

Fiskavaig: Short walk to a shingly bay.

Tarscavaig: Short walk to a lovely bay in Sleat.

Eyre Point: Pebble beach on the south end of Raasay.

1 Fairy Bridge

A quick scramble around one of the most scenic and magical spots on Skye.

This is a great place to get out of the car and stretch your legs. You can happily spend quarter of an hour wandering alongside the water, crossing and re-crossing the burn. The Gaelic name for this area is *Beul Atha nan Tri Allt*, 'The Ford of Three Burns'.

Where to start

Take the turning for Waternish from the main Portree/Dunvegan road (signposted for Stein), then take the left hand path just after you turn off the main road – this takes you down to an information and parking/turning area beside the old bridge.

Where to go

Take the old road that leads from the parking area over the bridge. You can scramble down from here to get to either side of the riverbank.

Time

A couple of minutes.

Path type

Old road and grassy bank.

Did you know?

The bridge is called after the fairy wife of a MacLeod chief who left her husband here on her return to the fairy world. She left the Fairy Flag behind her, now on display in the castle (see more on the story under Walk 5).

This area was a meeting place both during the Disruption, when open-air congregation meetings took place, and during the land reform agitation later in the nineteenth century. The crofters would gather here to listen to the speeches of John Macpherson, the Glendale Martyr, a crofter from Milovaig who was imprisoned in Edinburgh for his rebellious ways.

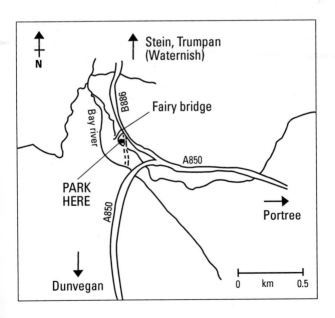

2   Glenbrittle Beach

Stroll to a wonderful beach in the shadow of the Cuillins.

A gorgeous spot to get out of the car, stretch your legs, enjoy the fresh air and soak up some absolutely glorious scenery.

Where to start

Drive down to the end of the road at Glenbrittle (a wonderful drive in the shadow of the Cuillins). Park just before the campsite; there is an overflow car park to the right (on the beach) if the car park is full.

Where to go

Walk through the dunes to the beach – then walk as long as you want along the beach and out onto the spit.

Time

2 minutes.

Path type

A walk along the beach.

Did you know?

Glenbrittle is one of the two main climbing bases in Skye. It is the starting point for one of the most well known 'short' walks in the mountains, to Coire Lagan. The views on the road down to Glenbrittle are spectacular, both of the Cuillins, and out to Rum and Canna.

There are toilets and a good shop at the campsite where you can get drinks, food and ice creams.

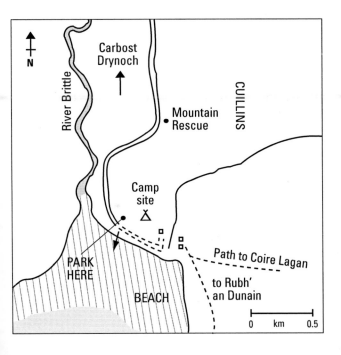

3 Beach near Staffin

Two minutes' walk to a gorgeous hidden beach.

The beach is narrow but was big enough for a family to be enjoying a game of cricket in the evening sun when I last visited. There are wonderful views from the shore across to Staffin Island, to the fairy knolls near Flodigarry, and out to Rona, Raasay and the mainland.

Where to start

Take the road from Portree to Staffin. Before you get to the cluster of houses at Staffin Bay take the minor road to the right for Staffin Slipway (also signposted for Quiraing Lodge and Boat Trips). Follow the road down towards the sea, cross the river to the right, then follow the road along until you get to a wide parking area looking out to Staffin Island.

Where to go

The path leads down from the parking area to the little beach below.

Time

Couple of minutes.

Path type

Grassy path.

Did you know?

In November 1884 the British Government sent two gunboats, a troopship, one hundred bluejackets and three hundred and fifty marines to deal with unrest on Skye associated with rent strikes and other action taken by the crofting community. A contingent of marines was marched cross-country from Uig to Staffin as a show of strength. The soldiers were quartered until the following year in Staffin Lodge.

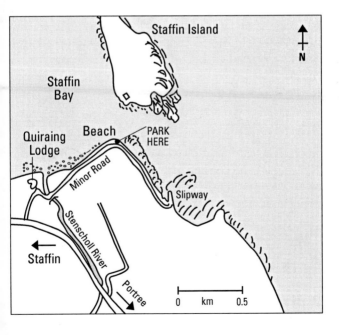

4   St John's Chapel, Caroy

Leafy churchyard at the head of a sea loch.

This is an extraordinarily peaceful and atmospheric spot. The churchyard is overgrown and the long grass is wet underfoot but this only adds to the feeling of being in a calm, green, leafy haven. It is worth visiting in the evening when the late sun throws a dappled light onto the headstones.

Where to start

Heading from Sligachan towards Dunvegan on the main road, the ruined chapel is just beyond the River Ose at the head of Loch Caroy. It is signposted from the road and there is a parking area just by the sign for St John's Chapel.

Where to go

There is a path leading down from the lay-by to the entrance of the churchyard. Proceed with a little care to wander around the church and graveyard (it is quite overgrown and uneven).

Time

Couple of minutes.

Path type

Good path to the start of the churchyard, however inside it is quite overgrown and may be very wet underfoot.

Did you know?

The Chapel of St John the Baptist and its churchyard were consecrated in 1838. It was built through the efforts of a few Episcopalian families led by MacLeod of Gesto. The story goes that he had shot a seal on a Sunday to the displeasure of the congregation and the minister of his church at Struan. The disagreement caused him to leave the church and set about building the chapel at Caroy.

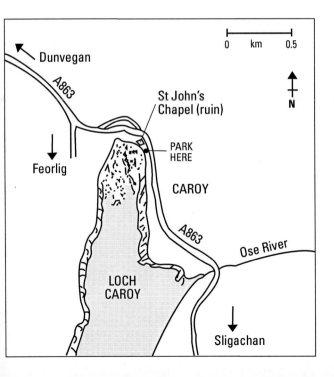

5   Dunvegan Castle Jetty

Panoramic views of the castle and sea loch.

All visitors eventually find themselves at Dunvegan
Castle and Gardens. For the best view of the castle,
make your way to the jetty at the seal boats. From here
you will enjoy panoramic views, normally in splendid
isolation.

Where to start

Park in the car park at the castle grounds. You need to
pay to get in to the castle and grounds, including the
jetty area.

Where to go

Make your way to the jetty at the seal boats, either
going down the road signposted for the boats or making your way to the sea from the castle gardens. With
the castle to your right there is a little path ahead that
takes you through some trees and out to the rocks at
the end.

Time

2 minutes from the jetty.

Path type

Slightly muddy path and rocks.

Did you know?

One of the most celebrated artefacts in the castle is the Fairy Flag. The story goes that the fairy wife of the fourth Chief of the MacLeods gave the flag to her husband upon her return to the fairy world. It was to bring good fortune to the clan: 'Keep this flag and unfurl it to the wind whenever a crisis hits you. It will save you and yours twice but woe betide you if you unfurl it a third time.' The flag, having been used twice (but not the third time) is now on display in the castle. The more prosaic story is that the flag was brought back from the Crusades. Most of us prefer the first version of events.

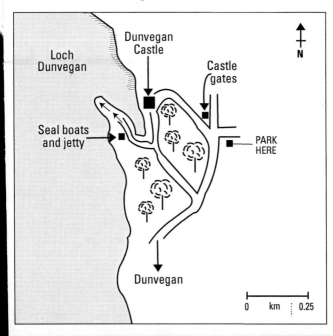

6   Hinnisdal River

Quick scramble to a river swimming pool and picnic spot.

This is one of my favourite spots on Skye. A quick scramble takes you down to a gorgeous rocky area by the river with beautiful scenery all around. On a good day you can swim in the river pools – if you don't fancy a dip it is still a great place to picnic, scramble or just sit and breathe in the view. It can be midgy later on in the day so pack midge repellent as well as swimming stuff and towels.

Where to start

Travelling from Borve to Uig take the road to the right signposted for Glenhinnisdal. Just under half a mile along the road you should be able to see the river and rocks down to your right. Park carefully at the edge of one of the passing places.

Where to go

Thick blue plastic has been wrapped around the top of the barbed wire fence at the start of the path: use this as a guide. There is a stile to help you over the fence. Follow the path through the bracken down to the rocks. From here you can take your time exploring, climbing over the rocks, paddling, swimming, sunbathing or picnicking.

On the way back look just upstream of the main rocks

to find the return path – it is a little hard to spot in the bracken.

Time

3 minutes.

Path type

Sheep track through grass and bracken.

Did you know?

The early Viking settlers called this river Hinnisdal, and its neighbour Romesdal, because they reminded them of the Norwegian rivers of the same name.

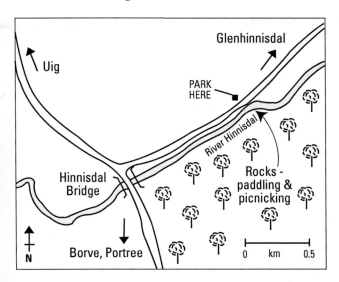

7　Fiskavaig

Short walk to a shingly bay.

This is a very easy walk down to the bay, offering wonderful views across to Healaval. It's a good place to sit and read, picnic, or scramble on the rocks.

Where to start

From Carbost, take the road towards Portnalong and keep going to Fiskavaig. You want to park about 0.6 miles after the sign for Fiskavaig, beyond a number of houses and the main bay you can see below you. Just before the road turns round to the right again there's a very wide passing place; park in the lay-by just beyond it on the left.

Where to go

Take the track going down to the right from the road. Once past the house on the right it turns into a clear grassy path through the bracken. This takes you straight down to the shore (shingly bay and rocks).

Time

3 minutes.

Path type

Grassy path, rocks.

Did you know?

The next township is Portnalong, where a number of families were settled by the Government after the First World War. Coming from over-populated areas in Lewis, Harris and Scalpay, they tried to make a living from weaving as well as crofting and fishing.

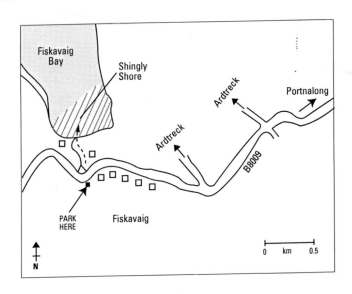

8   Tarscavaig

Short walk to a lovely bay in Sleat.

This is a very straightforward short walk. There are wonderful views from Tarscavaig to the Cuillins on a good day.

Where to start

Driving from Armadale towards Ord, take the left hand turn for Tarscavaig. Turn left again at the telephone box, head towards the sea and park (carefully) at the end of the road in the turning area.

Where to go

Walk along the track that continues at the end of the road. As you go through the gate you immediately find yourself at the side of the main bay; follow the path till it drops down to a ruined building. Keep on the path for another few minutes and you will find a choice of lovely spots to sit.

Time

5 minutes.

Path type

Cart track and grassy path.

Did you know?

The ruined building you go past at the shore was once a church. Writing in the 1920s Seton Gordon, in *The Charm of Skye*, described the small church built at the water's edge thus: '. . . during the Sabbath service the row of the surf mingles with the mournful cadences of the Gaelic psalms.'

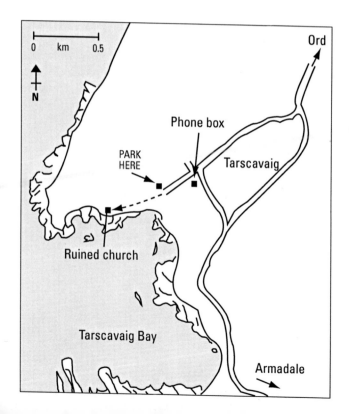

9 Eyre Point

Pebble beach on the south end of Raasay.

This is a beautiful, peaceful spot, miles from anywhere. It is a very short walk down to the beach but you can wander for long enough once you're there, soaking up the views back to the Cuillins and admiring the wondrous pebbles on the shore.

Where to start

From the Raasay ferry turn right and follow the road to the end. The views en route are stunning and there are a couple of good places to stop and look back at the mountains of Skye. Park in the lay-by on the right hand side just before the road end.

Where to go

Follow the path at the end of the road, bearing right when the path splits. When you see a break in the fencing to the right (after about five minutes) drop down to the shore. Walk along the pebbly beach as long as you like.

Time

5 minutes.

Path type

Grassy track then pebbles on the shore.

Did you know?

The houses beyond you are part of the township of Fearns. George Rainy cleared this area during the 1850s when the crofters were moved to the rocky north end of Raasay and Rona. In 1921 land raiders from Rona began rebuilding ruined houses at Fearns. They were imprisoned when they refused to relinquish the land.

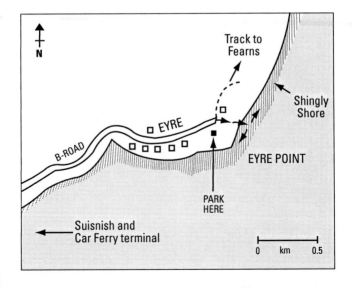

PART TWO

Quick History:
15 minutes and under

THIS SECTION OF short walks – all within 15 minutes – is aimed at exploring some of Skye's rich and fascinating history. These places are all well worth a visit. Their ruinous state only adds to the atmosphere – often spine-tinglingly so. Most are in wonderful settings that are worth walking to in their own right.

The section includes two road walks, suitable for those who find rough paths impossible: an easy stroll to some well preserved brochs and an exploration of some of Raasay's history. There are also four old churchyards, two ruined castles – one on the tourist trail, the other not – and the ruined crofting township at Galtrigill. I defy you not to hear the ghosts there.

Quick History includes:

Trumpan Church: Ruined church and graveyard with stunning views.

Cill Chriosd: Ruined church and churchyard in the shadow of the Red Cuillins.

Dunvegan Church: Old church and churchyard, including graves of the clan chiefs.

Galtrigill: Ruined crofting township in the north west of Skye.

St Columba's Isle: Ancient burial ground on a river island.

Duntulm Castle: Ruined castle in the north end of the island.

Glenelg Brochs: Easy walk to two well preserved brochs.

Knock Castle: Ruined castle with stunning views to the mainland.

Raasay House and surrounds: Easy road walk exploring Raasay's history.

10 Trumpan Church

Ruined church and graveyard with stunning views.

This walk takes you to the ruins of a church burned down as part of a terrible clan battle in the mid 16thc. It is well preserved, with an interesting churchyard. The church is at the far end of the Waternish peninsula and there are wonderful views across to the Outer Isles. It is a good spot to come in the evening and, if organised with a picnic supper, you could sit on the benches and watch the sun going down.

Where to start

Take the road to Waternish and keep going past Stein, following the signs to Hallin. From there keep going and follow the signs for Trumpan. Park in the large parking area opposite the ruined church.

Where to go

The churchyard is just over the road from the car park.

Time

Couple of minutes.

Path type

Grassy in the churchyard – may be wet underfoot.

Did you know?

In 1578 a group of MacDonalds sailed over to attack

the MacLeods at worship in the church. They burned the church to the ground, but one woman escaped to raise the alarm. A party of MacLeods arrived from Dunvegan and set about the MacDonalds. The tide had gone out, leaving their boats high and dry. Unable to retreat, the MacDonalds were killed. The sea wall was knocked over their corpses – and the incident is remembered as the Battle of the Spoiled Dyke.

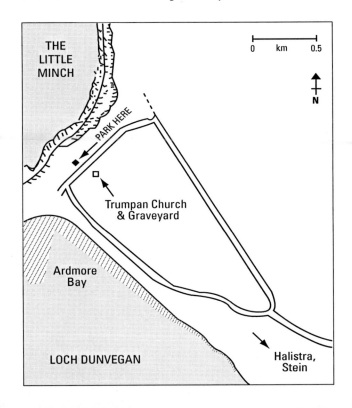

11 Cill Chriosd

Ruined church and churchyard in the shadow of the Red Cuillins.

The ruins at Cill Chriosd are of a church built in the late middle ages. This is a great place to stop if you are on your way down towards Elgol, with interesting ruins and a stunning setting.

Where to start

Take the road from Broadford to Elgol. A few miles along you will see the ruins of a church on the right hand side. There are a number of places where you can park here, including a lay-by just opposite the church.

Where to go

The churchyard is just over the road from the parking area.

Time

Couple of minutes.

Path type

Grassy path – easy access.

Did you know?

The mountain behind the church is *Beinn na Caillich* – Hill of the Old Woman. The old woman was reputedly 'Saucy Mary', who laid a chain between Kyle and Kyleakin to exact a toll from passing ships. The alternative version is that it refers to the remains of a Norwegian princess and that the cairn on top of the hill marks her grave.

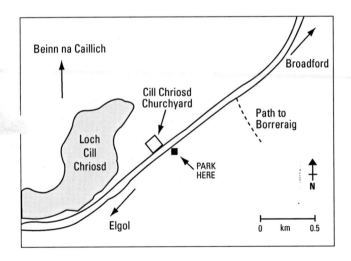

12 Dunvegan Church

Old church and churchyard, including graves of the clan chiefs.

This walk takes in the old church and churchyard at Dunvegan and, if you are feeling energetic, the hill just above it. Climbing the hill is both invigorating and rewarding, providing wonderful views of the village of Dunvegan, and across to Healaval and the Cuillins. The churchyard is well worth a visit, including grave-stones of a number of MacLeod clan chiefs and a plaque to the McCrimmons, hereditary pipers to the MacLeods.

Where to start

Heading out of Dunvegan on the Portree Road you will see the ruined church and churchyard on the hill on your left hand side. Park carefully just by a gate to the front of the churchyard.

Where to go

Walk up the grassy area to the churchyard. You can stop here if you want but it is worth climbing the hill behind you – you can use the memorial stone to guide you to the top.

Time

Couple of minutes. It's a five minute walk if you go up the hill.

Path type

Grass tracks to the churchyard and up the hill. The grass in the churchyard may be quite long, which will make it wet underfoot.

Did you know?

The stone on the top of the hill is a bit of modern rather than ancient history. It was placed there in 2000 to mark the Millennium.

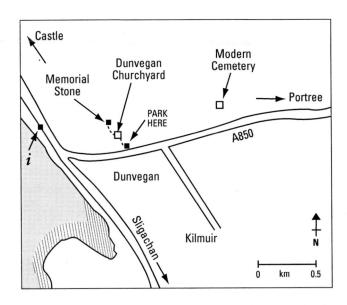

13 Galtrigill

Ruined crofting township in the north west of Skye.

Galtrigill is a wonderful spot to soak up some of the history and atmosphere of Skye. Although it is only a few minutes' 'walk' you can easily spend 15 to 20 minutes exploring the ruined buildings and listening to the ghosts of the past. The surviving buildings are in quite good condition and you can see the layout and building styles of the cleared township; you can also see evidence of lazy bed cultivation around the settlement.

Where to start

Take the road north from Colbost and take the right hand fork signposted Husabost. Follow the road to the end and park very carefully in the turning area – you must leave enough room for cars to turn.

Where to go

Take the path going off to the left from the turning place – it is quite clearly marked. You will soon see the outline of old ruined buildings with grass and wild flowers growing over them. You can wander about the area for a good while exploring the buildings and soaking up the atmosphere.

Time

5 minutes walking and anything up to 20 minutes exploring.

Path type

Grass and sheep tracks. The grass may be long and wet in places. You also need to take some care around the buildings as the long grass hides ditches and dykes that you might stumble into.

Did you know?

The beach you are looking across to is the Coral Beach – you may see the sand glinting white in the sunlight.

The township was abandoned because its peat moor lies some distance away with no road – living here must eventually have become too difficult without the means to invest and improve basic living conditions. Now only the ghosts are left.

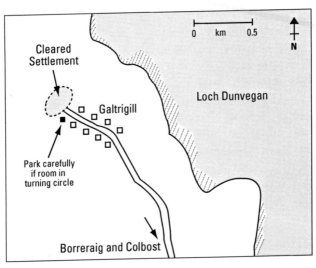

14 St Columba's Isle

Ancient burial ground on a river island.

This is a short walk to an ancient burial ground and the site of the cathedral church of the Bishops of the Isles. The chapel and churchyard are situated on an island in the River Snizort. With the construction of the bridge this is now an easy short walk to a spot that is both beautiful and absolutely reeking with history. If you can ignore the ghosts it would make a great spot to picnic (there is a bench conveniently situated at the river bank).

Where to start

Heading from Portree towards Dunvegan, as you approach Skeabost take the turning on the right for Uig, then turn first left. Park on the side of the road.

Where to go

The road takes you to the bridge over the River Snizort. Turn right here just before the bridge and follow the path along the river – you can see the outline of the ruined chapel on the island ahead. As you approach the wooden bridge there is a picnic area to the left. The path takes you to the bridge constructed in 1990, and leads you onto the islet.

There are many interesting headstones and flatstones in the churchyard and you could spend a good half hour exploring here.

Time

5 minutes.

Path type

Good, flat path; wooden bridge; thick (wet) grass in the graveyard.

Did you know?

This was an ancient burial ground and site of the cathedral church of the Bishops of the Isles from 1079 to 1498. You will also see the mortuary chapel of the Nicholsons of Scorrybreac where according to tradition 28 chiefs of the clan are buried.

In the early 16thc this area was the site of the Battle of Trotternish, one of the most important of Skye's clan wars (between the MacDonalds and MacLeods). There was a bloody battle at the ford of the river and the heads of the combatants were carried down the river, where they cumulated in a deep pool near the estuary known as *Coire nan Ceann* or 'Cauldron of the Heads'.

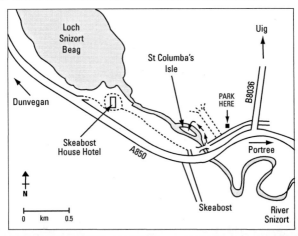

15 Duntulm Castle

Ruined castle in the north end of the island.

Duntulm Castle is a well known destination and you might find it a little touristy. There is not much left to see of the castle, although it is in an impressive spot and probably worth visiting for the setting as much as the ruin itself.

Where to start

Head north from Uig; take the left hand turn for Duntulm Castle Hotel and park in the car park (you can get a cup of tea in the hotel later).

Where to go

Follow the path that leads straight ahead of you from the car park, with the hotel to your right. Tulm Bay is ahead, with the ruins of Duntulm Castle ahead to your left.

Walk down to and then along the shore – there is no path here but if you follow the shoreline you will link up again with the path that snakes up the hill to the castle. Take the path up the cliff (proceeding with some care as it is quite a narrow path); this takes you to the ruins of the castle at the top.

Time

6 minutes.

Path type

Narrow path to shore and up hill (plus handrail); short walk along shore.

Did you know?

Duntulm is Gaelic for 'Fort on the Cliff'. The castle was originally a Pictish fortress, one of a chain of duns on the north coast. It became the residence of a Viking leader, then a MacDonald stronghold from the 13thC onwards. Legend has it that the MacDonalds left after a nurse dropped the chief's baby son from a window on to the rocks below.

In the bay lies Tulm Island and in clear weather *Fladda Chuain*, 'Fladda of the Ocean', can be seen. This is supposed to be the isle of perpetual youth, where it is said the sun never sets.

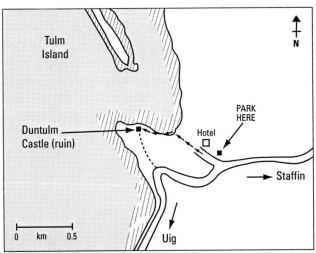

16 Glenelg Brochs

Easy walk to two well preserved brochs.

This walk is not on Skye but I have included it since it is a lovely detour if you are arriving by the Glenelg Ferry. (It is well worth taking the trip both for the fantastic scenery and to be able to arrive by boat. You can save the bridge for the drive back home.) The walk itself is a short, flat, easy walk on a minor road.

Where to start

From Glenelg turn left, signposted for the brochs, then left again. After 5 minutes on this road you will go over a cattle grid and should see the first broch on the right hand side. Park in the lay-by on the left.

Where to go

Cross over the road and go through the gate to the first broch. There is a grassy path that takes you into and around the broch. Once you have explored walk further down the glen along the minor road to the second broch. You can spend a good ten minutes at each broch exploring the ruins.

Time

8 minutes, plus time to explore at both brochs.

Path type

Minor road; grassy area around the two brochs.

Did you know?

The Glenelg ferry is the oldest ferry crossing to Skye. It was used by Boswell and Johnson when they visited in 1773, met on arrival on the other side by Flora MacDonald.

The first car ferry was two planks on a rowing boat. The 'Glenachulish' ferry that runs today can take up to six cars, with standing room for foot passengers. It takes about 5 minutes to cross – there is no timetable, with the boat running on demand. Remember though, the ferry service only operates in the summer months.

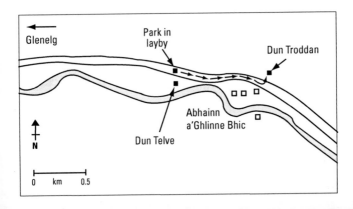

17 Knock Castle

Ruined castle with stunning views to the mainland.

This is a short but interesting walk. It takes you along the riverbank to the ruined castle on a lovely setting above Knock bay. There are magnificent views over the Sound of Sleat to the hills of Knoydart on the mainland.

Where to start

On the road to Armadale, take a turning to the left just before you come into Knock. The path is signposted for farm access. Park carefully just after you turn off the main road.

Where to go

Take the path heading past farm buildings on the left, keep going straight ahead (ignoring the path to the right), bear left and the path leads straight ahead. As you go down the hill take the path that branches off down to the left and cross the bridge going over the burn. Go through the small wooden gate to your right, which takes you onto a path through the trees. This path takes you through thick (wet) grass and tall bracken.

Once out in the open you will see the ruined castle ahead of you. When you reach the little jetty cut up to the left just beyond the boathouse and climb the sheep track up the hill. This takes you to a gap in the fence and an easy access route to the ruins.

Time

8 minutes.

Path type

Farm track then a narrow path through thick grass and bracken (potentially very wet underfoot); sheep track up to the castle.

Did you know?

These are the ruins of Castle Camus (better known by the later name of Knock Castle). It was a key stronghold of Sleat and for a time it was the chief stronghold of the MacDonalds, Lords of the Isles. By 1690 it was uninhabited and is now a ruin.

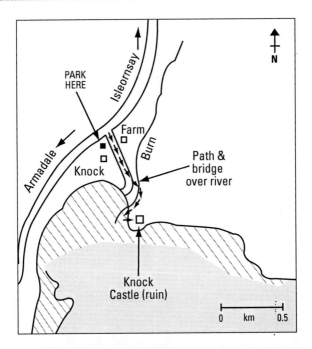

18 Raasay House and surrounds

Easy road walk exploring Raasay's history.

This is an easy but rewarding walk that takes you to a number of points of historical interest on Raasay and gives you a real sense of the ancient and modern history of the island. It also includes a detour to a beautiful bay and a tearoom, so there is something for all tastes!

Where to start

Drive towards Inverarish from the ferry and follow signs for the Outdoor Centre. Just before the turning into the Centre itself park somewhere near the semi-derelict stables block – there should be plenty of room.

Where to go

Walk along the road in the direction you've come from. The first thing you come to is the ruined chapel and graveyard at St Moluag's. A few minutes further along the road you will come to a pictish symbol stone (off the road to the right, through a little iron gate).

If you want a pleasant detour on a nice day, cross over the road and take the path going down to the left. This takes you towards the bay – and drops you right down to the shore from a little track just beyond the bench. Enjoy wonderful views across to Trotternish from here. Back up from the bay, retrace your steps to the road.

At this point (just across the road from the pictish stone) take the path down to Raasay House – now the

Outdoor Centre. Stop in the house for coffee. Then drop down to the bay and jetty in front of you, exploring (with some amazement) the outrageous mermaid statues at the gun battery. Pick up the tarmac road running along the shore then turn left up the hill back to the stables block and your car.

Time

About 15 minutes to the half way point, plus time exploring at the churchyard and bay.

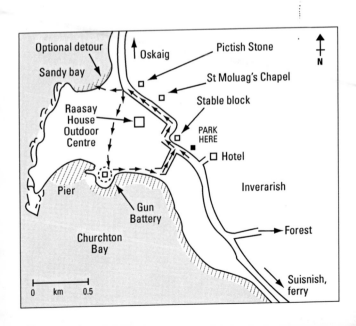

Path type

Tarmac and grassy paths; the path to the bay is a little muddy.

Did you know?

The original Raasay House was destroyed in 1750. The efforts of the MacLeod family to rebuild it – including some over-elaborate features like the mermaids – got them into massive debts, leading them to sell up and emigrate. The estate was bought up by George Rainy, responsible for the mass programme of clearances in the 1850s.

At the start of World War I soldiers leaving Raasay for France gathered under the clock at the stables block. It is said that the clock stopped then and never worked again. Of the 36 men that left only 12 returned.

PART THREE

Walks on the Wild Side: 20 minutes and under

THIS IS PROBABLY my favourite type of walk on Skye. They are not too long – within 25 minutes – but they are all well off the beaten track, mainly with no path to follow. You will fall down ditches, clamber up hills, plough your way through bracken, scramble over rocks, and pull your feet out of bogs; you will no doubt get tired, scratched, bitten and soaked – but you will be rewarded by getting to places of solitude, wild magic and beauty, with a real sense of personal achievement.

This section includes an obvious cheat in the walk to Loch Coruisk. It *is* one of Skye's wildest places but this route takes you there by boat and a reasonably clear path, not through the mountains. You are likely to be accompanied by a crowd of fellow travellers rather than awestruck on your own. But the other walks may well be done in splendid isolation – I didn't see a soul on any of them.

Four of the walks take you to rocky bays and headlands. Three – probably my favourite trio of the whole book – take you out to the ruins of ancient forts on headlands jutting out into Skye's sea lochs. You will feel a fantastic sense of wonder and achievement when you find them for yourself.

Try out:

Camus a Mhor Bheoil: Shingly bay with wonderful views of Trotternish.

Roag Island: Sheep tracks to tidal island in Loch Bracadale.

Uiginish: Hidden bay with stunning views to Dunvegan Castle.

Loch Coruisk: Boat trip and short walk to the heart of the Cuillins.

Dun Ardtreck: Wild walk to the ruins of an ancient fort.

Dun Ringill: Exciting walk to an old fort on the edge of Loch Slappin.

Dun Fiadhairt: Well preserved broch on the shores of Loch Dunvegan.

Camus Ban: Exciting walk to a hidden bay looking out to Raasay.

19 Camus a Mhor Bheoil

Shingly bay with wonderful views of Trotternish.

This is a lovely short walk, rewarding you with wonderful views to Trotternish and Raasay, and a long stretch of shingly bay where you can sit, explore and picnic at your leisure. There is no path as such but it is easy enough to follow your nose down to the bay. You could walk for longer around the bay if you wanted to – it would certainly be a good place for kids to scramble about.

Where to start

Heading out from Portree to Sligachan, take the left hand turn for the Braes. After about 10 minutes take the left hand turn for Gedintailor and Balmeanach. A few minutes along this road (and before the sign for Balmeanach) you will see a large gravelled area on the left hand side where you can park. You can see the bay and spit beyond you.

Where to go

From the parking area walk across the grassy (and slightly boggy) moorland. Bear right towards the bay. Look for a sheep track to the right that takes you along the side of some trees and bushes at the top of the hill above the bay. Follow this sheep track along and down towards the bay (it is a little steep in places). Then meander down to the rocks and from there to the silvery black bay.

When you retrace your steps you are aiming for the sheep track that you can see snaking up the hill. Once you are at the top just head back over the grassy area towards the houses ahead of you.

Time

9 minutes.

Path type

Grass, sheep tracks, rocks.

Did you know?

The road to this walk takes you past the site of the Battle of the Braes, where in April 1882 the crofters of this area, who were protesting about their conditions, came into conflict with government forces. There is a memorial stone marking the spot and commemorating their actions just past the township of Ollach.

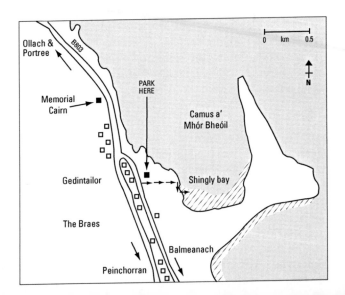

20 Roag Island

Sheep tracks to tidal island in Loch Bracadale.

This is a perfect late afternoon walk when the evening light transforms the landscape. The walk is included in this 'wild' section since it takes you over rough ground with only a sheep track to follow. It would however be pretty difficult to get lost – all you have to do is follow your nose out to the headland. From here there are panoramic views of Loch Bracadale and surrounds, taking in the Cuillins, Healaval, MacLeod's Maidens (the stacks out to sea), with Canna sitting calmly on the horizon.

Where to start

From the main Sligachan to Dunvegan Road turn left for Roag. As you go through the strung out row of houses take the minor road to the left just opposite the post box – it is signposted for Ardroag, but the sign is barely visible. Follow the road down to the shore. Park safely just off the road near the cattle grid – just before the sign indicating no parking or dogs beyond this point.

Where to go

Keep following the tarmac road past a house and well cared for garden on the left hand side but then take the path going straight ahead of you rather than the continuation of the road round to the left. Follow this good path which then peters out to a sheep track. You are really just following your nose here towards the headland and out to sea. The sheep track takes you to the narrow tidal causeway and up the hill on the other side. Make your way from here over fairly rough ground to the far end of the island.

Time
About 15 minutes walking but you may well spend longer exploring the shoreline.

Path type
Minor road then sheep track; walk over rocks and seaweed to cross the causeway.

Did you know?
The Viking Haco arrived here in 1263 with a fleet of galley ships after the Battle of Largs. When his soldiers landed they despoiled the surrounding countryside.

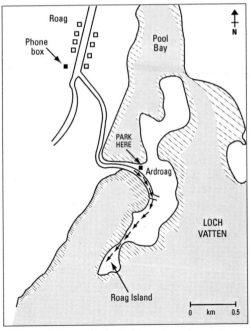

21 Uiginish

Hidden bay with stunning views to Dunvegan Castle.
This is a lovely short walk to a hidden bay which you
will most likely have all to yourself. (The only company
I had was a seal basking next to me on the rocks.) There
is no path as such other than a sheep track. From the
shore you gain a wonderful vantage point over the short
stretch of water to Dunvegan Castle.

Where to start

Take the road from Dunvegan towards Glendale and
turn right at the sign for Uiginish lodge (with a very
distinctive owl marking the turning point!). Follow the
road along for five minutes and park carefully near
the farm buildings at the end of the road.

Where to go

Go past the large lodge on your right hand side, then
through the gate, which takes you to a farm track heading out to sea. Follow this path and you will see the castle to your right. After a little while you will come to a
gap in the fence (and a couple of gates to your left); go
through the gap and follow the sheep track out to sea.
Follow the track as it descends and you will see the little
bay below you. Clamber down the side of the hill to the
rocks at the bottom. There is a lovely bay where you can
sit – you can also follow the rocks around to the right to
explore the coastline further.

To return simply retrace your steps from the bay back
up the hill. Bear right when you get up the hill to take
you to the ridge – the sheep track from here will lead
you to the gap in the fence and eventually back to the
farmhouse.

Time

15 minutes, plus however long you spend exploring at the rocks.

Path type

Farm and sheep tracks, some scrambling through grass, heather and bracken. Potentially wet underfoot.

Did you know?

In January 1883 a steamer was sent into Loch Dunvegan carrying 50 policemen – an attempt by the authorities to quell growing civil unrest and protest over land rights and living conditions. The crofters heard that the ship was on its way and gathered in the village in protest. The police retreated from the crowd – consisting mainly of youths and boys carrying sticks – and took refuge in the castle.

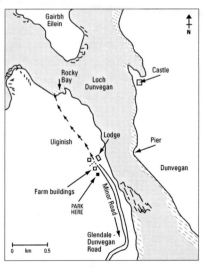

22 Loch Coruisk

Boat trip and short walk to the heart of the Cuillins.

I am cheating slightly to include this as a 'wild' walk since you (unlike the dedicated hikers) access this area of remote wilderness by boat. But this is a 'must do' trip for any visitor to Skye. The views from Elgol to the Cuillins are stunning; the 45 minute boat trip is rewarding in itself; and the short walk at Loch Coruisk takes you into the heart of the Cuillins at its wildest. The only slight downside of the trip is that you don't have long enough at the loch to explore. If you want to arrange a longer trip you can walk a lot further – but that takes you beyond the remit of this book.

Where to start

Take the road from Broadford to Elgol. Park at the end of the road in the car park above the jetty; if this is full there is another car park back up the hill (there are also public toilets there). From the jetty take the *Bella Jane* boat trip to Loch Coruisk. This is a very popular trip so you will need to book in advance.

Where to go

The boat takes you to a landing point at Loch Scavaig. You will be directed from the boat to the path that runs alongside the river flowing out of Loch Coruisk. After about 5 minutes you will see the loch ahead of you. You have two choices here, either go over the stepping stones to your right or follow the path round to the left.

Going over the stepping stones is a slightly better option, giving you better views and a good place to swim if you're up for it. You need to take care going over the stones but it is a good crossing and the stones don't move at all when you step on them. Follow the path up the hill and round to the left – keep up at this point or you'll drop down to the waterside too soon. After about 10 minutes you will see a little bay below you. You can walk down here and admire the view down the loch or go for a swim.

If you don't want to cross the stones you can walk around the other side of the loch. The path on this side is, however, a lot more boggy and you can only do it with good boots.

If you don't fancy the walk or have good boots, fear not! You can walk just a few minutes and stop on the left-hand side of the loch just above the stepping stones. The views from here are still breathtaking.

Time

About 15 minutes. Remember to leave yourself enough time to get back to the boat.

Path type

Rocks and stepping stones, and a narrow rocky path; boggy ground if you walk round to the west of the loch.

Did you know?

Loch Coruisk, the 'Corrie or Cauldron of Water', lies at the head of Loch Scavaig. It was scooped out of the solid rock by ice 280,000 years ago. It is the most famous corrie in Britain, much written about and over-romanticised. Alexander Smith in his book *A Summer in Skye* (a great companion guide to the island) described it as follows:

'the most savage scene of desolation in Britain. Conceive a large lake filled with dark green water, girt with torn and shattered precipices, the bases of which are strewn with ruin since an earthquake passed that way and whose summits jag the sky with grisly splinter and peak.'

Go and see it for yourself!

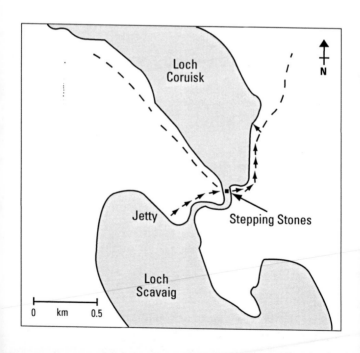

23 Dun Ardtreck

Wild walk to the ruins of an ancient fort.

This walk is not long but it is demanding – there is no path and much of the ground is very wet or uneven. But if you don't mind sinking unexpectedly into ditches or bogs it could be for you! You are rewarded with the ancient ruins of the dun, situated in a wild and beautiful spot on the edge of Loch Bracadale, perched upon a stack of rock rearing 50 feet above the shore. You are very unlikely to meet anyone else on your travels and if you want to linger there is a hidden bay where you can sit and watch the sea.

Where to start

Take the road from Carbost towards Portnalong, bearing left for Fiskavaig. Before you reach Fiskavaig take the first road to the right signposted for Adrtreck. Drive to the end of the road and park carefully, either at the very edge of the turning area (but leaving room for turning) or just off the road.

Where to go

This is a hard walk to describe, as there is no path. You will however be able to construct your own route once you have spotted the broch – you just need to keep making towards it.

Take the path going off to the right from the turning area (not the better path going straight ahead at the end of the road). Follow this cart track and go over the first gate (1). On a good day you will see Healaval ahead of you. Follow the path slightly down hill and round to the right, towards a farmhouse and farm building with a red roof. The path takes you to a double gate. Take the gate (2) to the left and keep going straight ahead. This takes you through fairly boggy ground. Follow the sheep tracks slightly further on. After about five minutes from the start you should see the dun before you and slightly to the left, with Healaval behind it.

You should see a fence ahead. It might be useful to climb up slightly to look for a spot to get through or over the fence – from higher ground you should be able to see a gate ahead of you. Head for that – it takes another couple of minutes to reach it.

Over the gate (3) keep going straight, following the sheep tracks towards Healaval, over fairly rough ground. You will end up walking through quite thick grass, passing between two low ridges on either side. When you get to the end of these ridges (about 10 minutes from the start of the walk) turn left and you will see the dun ahead of you. Take care though! You need to keep your eyes on the ground, not the dun, as the ground is very uneven and boggy.

When you get through this stretch of ground climb up the hill to the broch – it is in good condition and you can explore in and around it.

On the way back down you can take a little detour by climbing down to the lovely little bay to your left. Otherwise just retrace your steps back down the hill, through the area of uneven and boggy ground, then

right again in a gap between two ridges. Head for the
knoll ahead of you then bear slightly left at the knoll
– from here you should see a gate (3). Go though the
gate and from here head towards the corrugated iron
farm building. You will see the double gate in front of
you – head towards it, using the farm building to
guide you. Once over the gate (2) turn right along the
good path, which will take you back to the last gate
(1) and from there to the road.

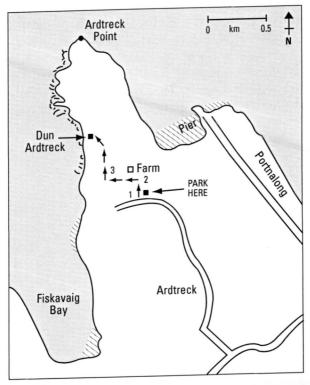

Time

About 18 minutes, but you might need to meander a bit to find your way.

Path type

Very uneven ground; quite difficult to walk through; wet and muddy underfoot.

Did you know?

Duns were fortified round towers built in the Iron Age. Many were still in use when the Norsemen began their raids. It is thought that some may have been up to 40 or 50 feet high, with small galleries between the inner and outer walls. The duns were all in view of other duns or brochs, providing an effective means of communication.

24 Dun Ringill

Exciting walk to an old fort on the edge of Loch Slappin.

This walk takes you along a beautiful stretch of coastland to the hidden remains of an old fort. The scenery is stunning all the way, with fantastic views across Loch Slappin and Loch Eishort and out to sea.

Where to start

From the Broadford to Elgol road take the turning to the left, signposted Kilmarie churchyard. Drive down to the sea and park in the grassy area just as the road turns round to the right.

Where to go

Walk back along the road; just as you pass the entrance to the big house you'll see a gate on the right. Go through the gate and follow the path to a lovely bridge over the river. Cross the bridge and turn up and right – this path takes you through the woods to another gate, then alongside the river to the shore. Cut up to the left through the grass to a stile – this takes you to a reasonable sheep path which goes all the way to the dun.

The fort may not be immediately apparent – what you will see after about 20 minutes' walking is three smallish headlands out to your right. As you get closer you will see that the middle one has been fortified. You can go right up and almost into it although it is very overgrown.

Follow the same track on the way back. When the path forks after about 10 minutes (just above the sandy stretch of the bay) take the lower path to the left, which will take you back to the stile. Cut down towards the shore and cross the little stream before the path takes you back into the woods, over the bridge and back to the road.

Time

20 to 25 minutes.

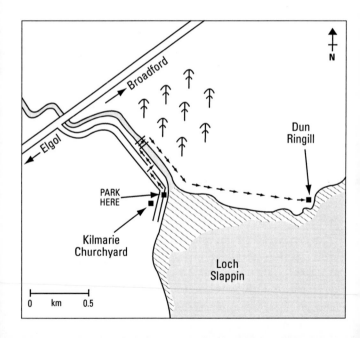

Path type

Mainly a sheep track – boggy and quite uneven in places, and you need to go through tall grasses and bracken.

Did you know?

Dun Ringill was originally the Mackinnon stronghold – thought to have been occupied as early as the 9thC. It is said that they protected the kyle (Gaelic *caol*, 'straight of water') from here, sailing out and exacting a toll from passing ships.

25 Dun Fiadhairt

Well preserved broch on the shores of Loch Dunvegan

This is another favourite, taking you to a little known but well preserved broch in a stunning location. Finding it is like stumbling across a piece of hidden magic.

It is not a difficult walk but there is no obvious path and the terrain is quite rough in places. Be prepared to get scratched or soaked or both – but also to be rewarded with a wonderful piece of history and a beautiful spot to explore. You could extend the trip by stopping for a while at Camalaig Bay – to read, picnic or just soak in the view.

Where to start

Head north out of Dunvegan, past the castle car park, then follow signs for Claigan (and the coral beach). There are lovely views out across the loch from this road. As you approach the crossing over Loch Suardal turn right onto a grassy area by a gate at the side of the road, just before you go over the water. Park carefully, leaving gate access. (NB the loch is largely covered in grasses so it isn't immediately recognisable as the large stretch of water you might be expecting from the OS map.)

Where to go

The directions for this walk are quite detailed – partly because there is no path, partly because it falls into a number of short sections rather than one long stretch. I hope it does not make it sound over-complicated. It is much easier to find than it is to describe – honestly!

Go along the road crossing the water. Take the path to your left just over the bridge and climb over the gate. Follow the path up the hill. After a minute or so take the right hand fork; this takes you through some quite thick grass. You need to make your way here as best you can – there is no clear path, you are heading for the dry stone wall ahead and a clear dip between two small ridges over to the left. You will go through that dip, so make for that general direction.

After another few minutes you will be clear of the long grass. Turn left to the dip between the ridges. There is a track ahead going straight towards the sea which you should follow. On a good day you will see Healaval in front of you but don't rely on it as a guide if the cloud is thick!

After another five minutes or so you will get to the top of the hill and see the splendour of the loch ahead of you. There is a field of bracken below you – the trick is to take the sheep track to your right going along the side of the hill. This takes you above the bracken rather than having to plough through it.

After another five minutes – about fifteen minutes into the walk – the sea to the Outer Isles comes into view. You should at this point be able to see the broch in the distance – it is a grey, honeycomb-shaped building.

Heading in the general direction of the broch as you drop down you will see that you need to cross a causeway to reach your destination. Make your way through the bracken towards the causeway, picking up a path to the left that takes you to the sea.

Once over the causeway head up hill towards

Healaval. Climb up to the right to get your bearings –
you should see the broch directly ahead of you. The only
route from here is through fairly thick grass and bog
cotton – so potentially quite wet underfoot. Once over
the boggy ground climb round to the right of the broch
to the entranceway. You can go all the way in but proceed with care – it's very uneven underfoot and so overgrown it is hard to see what you are walking on.

You will no doubt want to spend some time exploring
this wonderful site. When you are ready to leave go
back over the boggy ground and up through the
bracken. You will see the sea below you with a track
ahead bearing down to the left – this takes you down
to Camalaig Bay, a wonderful spot to sit and soak in
the beauty of your surrounds.

From here go back up to the causeway and turn left.
Head up hill, following the path through the bracken,
towards a dry stone wall. Cut slightly up to the right
to take you through a gap in the wall, then pick up the
sheep track again, going along the side of the hill. You
should be able to see the castle ahead of you now. The
track takes you above the large field of bracken you
can see, then down hill slightly until you cut left to go
back through the gap in the two ridges.

You should see the road ahead of you. Bear right and
pick up what you can of the sheep tracks. The grass is
quite thick here though, so it is not always clear where
the path is. Keep making for the loch and the road
ahead; you will eventually cut down to the left and
pick up the cart track back to the gate and the road.

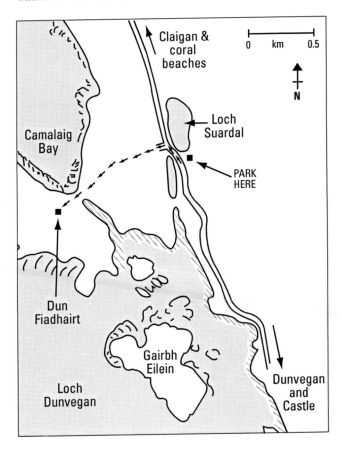

Time

20 minutes, plus time to explore the broch, and sit at the bay.

Path type

Sheep track, thick grass and bog, bracken.

Did you know?

The broch was excavated in 1914, when amongst other things an amber necklace was found. A terra cotta model of a bale of goods of Roman origin was also uncovered – supposed to be protection against bad luck on a journey.

The broch is well preserved and you can get a good sense of its size and structure. From inside, the main wall towers above you at about eight or nine feet. Take your time to explore the building – the entrance-way, galleries, stairwell and inner and outer walls.

26 Camus Ban

Exciting walk to a hidden bay looking out to Raasay.

This is a pretty wild walk: the ground is wet in places and rough in others – and the last section takes you down a steep hill through very thick bracken. The reward is a secret bay, with a wide sandy beach, good places to paddle, and even a net for volleyball!

Where to start

Heading out from Portree to Sligachan, take the left hand turn for the Braes, then turn left again for Penifiler. Continue along to the end of the road. Either park very carefully in the turning area (leaving room for turning) or just before it on the side of the road, leaving room for cars and farm vehicles to get past.

Where to go

Go through the gate at the end of the road. Follow the tarmac road as far as the large blue house near the shore. Walk in front of the house, then down on to the edge of the rocks to walk along the side of the wall.

At the end of the farm wall turn right (following the line of the wall) and climb up the hill. You are following a water course so some of this entails climbing over rocks that may be wet. It is a little tricky to climb but not a great distance. At the top keep going ahead over grass and slightly boggy moorland to reach the top of the hill. (There is no path – just follow your nose.) At the top you will see Camus Ban below you. Make your way down towards the bay. The last section is tricky as you climb through the bracken down a fairly steep slope. Watch out for holes and ditches – it would be easy to disappear! Once you emerge from the bracken you are at the edge of the wide sandy bay. Go back by retracing your steps up through the bracken

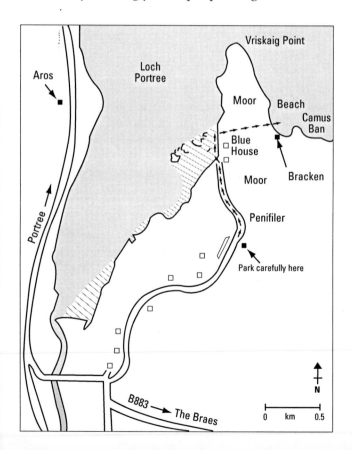

and over the grassy moor. Bear slightly to the left of a clump of bushes and trees on the top of the hill to pick up the rocky path back down to the shore. Going this way you can use the red building of Aros on the other side of the bay as a guide to make for all the way back to the blue house. Take care going back down the hill; it may be slippery.

Time

20 to 25 minutes.

Path type

Minor road; shore line; sheep tracks; grass; moorland; some boggy area; bracken; sandy beach (a bit of everything in fact!).

Did you know?

Camus Ban means 'Fair Bay' in Gaelic. The sand is actually slightly black but it is a wonderful flat beach, perfect for children to play on if you can get them down there!

PART FOUR

Highways to Heaven: 40 minutes and under

THIS SECTION CONTAINS the longest walks – although all can be done in less than 40 minutes. These walks have relatively clear paths so are easier to follow – but are not necessarily easy walking. Some go quite steeply up and down hill (the walk at Borreraig takes you up and down a cliff).

That being said many of these walks are very straightforward and are good to do with children – in particular the walks at Talisker, Neist Point, Loch Bharcasaig, Kylerhea and Loch Losait. If you are lucky enough to get good weather head for the beaches at Talisker and Loch Bharcasaig – both easy, flattish walks taking you to beaches and rocks where you can sunbathe and swim all day.

Some of the walks are off the tourist trail – the walk at Loch Niarsco for example just happened to be the path from my front door. Some are well known and may be busy. Most of the walks, as in the other sections, are focused on the coastline of Skye, but I have included two that take you into the mountain areas, offering lovely river walks and stunning views of the Cuillins.

The last walk of the section and of the book is to Hallaig – quite a drive to the starting point, and quite a long walk, but well worth it both for the glorious views and the sense of place and history that you will feel when you get there.

Portree Forest: Straightforward forest walk.

Bearreraig Bay: Demanding cliff walk to a bay under the Old Man of Storr.

Fairy Pools: Easy walk into the heart of the Cuillins.

Neist Point: Exhilarating walk to the most westerly point on Skye.

Loch Bharcasaig: Forest track to a beautiful beach with stunning views.

Allt Dearg: Riverside walk in the foothills of the Cuillins.

Ord: Easy walk to a lovely bay on the edge of Loch Slappin.

Talisker Bay: Easy walk to a gorgeous beach and picnic spot.

Kylerhea Otter Hide: Forest walk to an otter hide.

Loch Losait: Explore one of the most secluded bays on Skye.

Trumpan Headland: A glorious walk along the Waternish headland.

Loch Niarsco: A walk across the moor.

Oronsay: Straightforward walk to a tidal island in Loch Bracadale.

Hallaig: Stunning coastal walk with poetry, cleared houses and memories – the inspiration for Sorley Mac-Lean's famous poem.

27 Portree Forest

Straightforward forest walk.

This is a well-publicised Forestry Commission walk. Although a good path, it is steep in places and might not suit all levels of fitness. The shade of the trees can provide welcome relief on a hot day but they do restrict your view – apart from the lovely viewing area above the bay where you can stop for a while at the picnic benches. Not an inspiring walk but worth doing if you are also taking in the exhibition area at Aros (or just stopping there for refreshments).

Where to start

Head out from Portree towards Sligachan. Turn right just beyond the no speed limit sign as you leave the town – signposted for Aros Experience. Park in the visitor centre car park.

Where to go

The forest walk is signposted from the car park, heading straight up into the woods. The path climbs quite steeply at first before levelling off after about five minutes. It then takes you round to the left, then right and up hill again. After another five minutes or so you will see a clear path back down to the left and start the descent back down the hill. This takes you to the picnic area, with lovely views across Loch Portree.

Follow the path back down again. It forks occasionally as you meander through the forest but don't worry too much about which route to take – they all connect up in the end. The path will eventually bring you back to the car park.

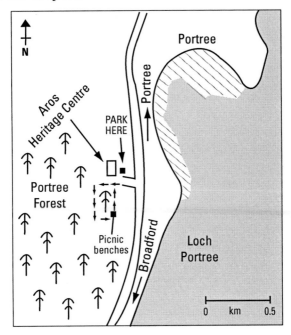

Time

15 minutes to the viewing area (roughly the half way point).

Path type

Forest track.

Did you know?

The Forestry Commission has constructed another short walk here based on the trees of the Gaelic alphabet. This isn't a great walk but it is an interesting insight into an element of Gaelic culture which was closely intertwined with the natural environment. Trees were used to represent the letters as a way of teaching the alphabet to children – so A was *Ailm* or elm and B was *Beith* or birch and so on.

28 Bearreraig Bay

Demanding cliff walk to a bay under the Old Man of Storr.

This walk takes you down a steep cliff to a wonderful bay surrounded by amazing cliffs and great views out to Raasay, Rona and Applecross. It is not easy to take in the views though: on the way down you need to concentrate on your footing, and on the way back up all you can see is the cliff looming ahead of you!

It is an area of particular interest to geologists and the bay is said to be good for fossils. If you are just looking to end up at a wonderful bay however, there are other easier walks that you could try.

Where to start

Take the road from Portree to Staffin. Just before the Old Man of Storr you will see the Storr Lochs on your right hand side. At the sign for the power station take the minor road to your right. Drive down to the power station, going carefully over the dam, and park at the building at the top of the small railway serving the power station.

Where to go

There is a signposted path taking you round to the right of the building and through a gate. This takes you down to a viewing and information area – there is a lot of useful information on the visitor board and good views of the cliffs.

There is a path leading off down the hill to the right of the viewing area. Follow this path all the way down to the bay below you. Take care!! The path is narrow, steep and very slippery in places. I don't like heights and had to tiptoe my way slowly down the hill. It was easier going up – at least from that point of view – but it was quite a hard slog climbing the 120 or so metres back up the cliff!

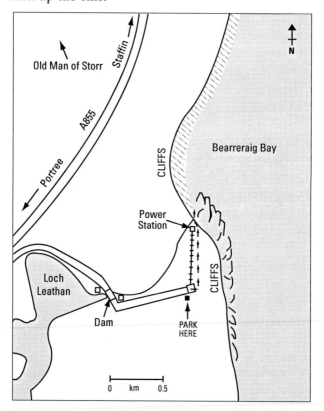

Time

About 20 minutes going down (if you are surefooted you could do it a lot quicker) and 15 minutes coming back up.

Path type

Narrow and steep path. There are rocks to stop the path eroding but these can in themselves be quite slippery. (NB for previous visitors to Skye – you can no longer walk up and down the 640 steps at the side of the railway – public access is now denied for safety reasons).

Did you know?

A fishing boat on the Storr Lochs was used to get Bonnie Prince Charlie off the island. Two men carried the boat down the cliff and got him away to Raasay. However hard you find the walk just be thankful you're not carrying a boat down with you!

29 Fairy Pools

Easy walk into the heart of the Cuillins.

This is a lovely short walk taking in some beautiful mountain scenery without the need to climb too far. The fairy pools – deep, turquoise blue pools – are an unusual feature and a good place to stop and picnic, or just to dip your toes into the magic water. It is a straightforward path all the way, offering an easy and accessible route into the splendour of the Cuillins.

Where to start

Take the road from Carbost to Glenbrittle. About 10 minutes down the road you will see a parking area on the right hand side. Turn in here and park – you should see a sign marking the start of a path for Loch Eynort. Cross the main road and head towards the green sign marking the path to Sligachan.

Where to go

Follow the path signposted for Sligachan but only for a minute until the path splits – take the right hand path going down the hill. Keep to it all the way down and then up again towards the mountains, following the course of the river all the way. You need to cross small burns and the river a couple of times but these are easy crossings and (non-slippery) stepping stones. The path takes you up to a series of waterfalls and deep water pools – the fairy pools.

Time

18 minutes, plus time exploring the falls and pools.

Path type

Clear track all the way.

Did you know?

The last major battle between the MacDonalds and the MacLeods was fought in this area – Coire na Creiche – in 1601. This conflict was started when a MacDonald chief sent his wife – the sister of a MacLeod chief – back home after she lost the sight of an eye. The insult was compounded by sending her home on a one-eyed horse led by a one-eyed boy and accompanied by a one-eyed dog. The 'war of the one-eyed woman' lasted for two years and ended here.

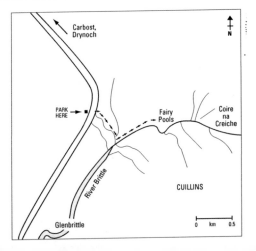

30 Neist Point

Exhilarating walk to the most westerly point on Skye.

This is a fun walk on a good path that climbs and descends steeply. It's a good one to do with kids. The lighthouse and cliffs make a fantastic viewpoint at the end and there are wonderful rocks where you can scramble an hour or so away.

Where to start

Take the road up out of Glendale and follow signs for Neist Point. Follow this road to the end – you will either see a space for parking at the end or, if it is busy, you will need to park carefully just off the road.

Where to go

Walk up to the low lying building near the gate – the path takes you round the left hand side of the wall – you will see the main path leading off in front of you. Follow this all the way down the cliff and up again towards the lighthouse.

After 15 to 20 minutes you will reach the perimeter of the lighthouse – you need to cut left here to go round the fence (it is quite muddy here) and round to the rocks. You can spend a good long time exploring the rocks – if you keep wandering round away from the lighthouse you will end up at a rocky/sandy beach (close to the iron jetty). This is a lovely spot to explore, with rock pools where the kids can scramble.

From here head back towards the lighthouse (over the

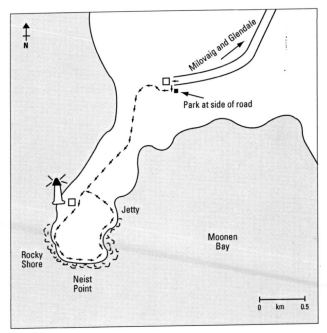

grass) then pick up the main path again, going back up the hill.

Time

15 minutes going down (20 minutes coming back up!) plus at least 20 minutes exploring at the rocks.

Path type

A good tarmac path all the way – steep in places but with steps and a handrail to guide you. Rocks to scramble over at the end.

Did you know?

This is the most westerly point on Skye, with some of
the steepest cliffs. The lighthouse was built in 1908 and
manned until 1989. You get wonderful views from here
to the Outer Isles on a good day – but it is also quite
an exposed spot and many a time I've done this walk
in the cold, wind and rain. None of that diminishes
the magic.

31 Loch Bharcasaig

Forest track to a beautiful beach with stunning views.

This is a simple walk on a clear forest track all the way to the shore. It would make a good walk with kids as it is flat all the way and takes you to a sandy bay where you can swim on a good day or scramble about on the rocks and poke around at the remains of crabs and jellyfish. The views both en route and from the bay are out of this world.

Where to start

Take the road to Glendale from near Dunvegan, then the left hand fork for Orbost. Follow the road down to the end (going past the sign for the gallery) and park in the large parking area in front of Orbost House, next to the farm buildings.

Where to go

Take the path to the right hand side of Orbost House, signposted for Idrigill Point. Follow this good forest track all the way to the shore – as you get near the beach you need to walk behind the old sheep pens and over/through the gate, before you drop down to the black sands.

Time

20 minutes.

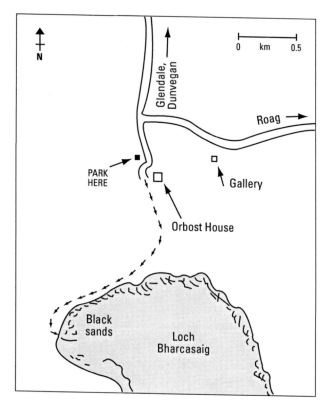

Path type

Good, clear forest track (good enough for a buggy, I think).

Did you know?

Orbost House was the home of Otta Swire, who wrote the wonderful book, *Skye: the Island and its Legends*.

(If you don't have a copy buy one – it makes a great companion to your holiday). She reports in her book that the sands were once white – they are supposed to have turned black in a single night of a storm.

32 Allt Dearg

Riverside walk in the foothills of the Cuillins.

Allt Dearg is Gaelic for Red Burn: a beautiful river that you follow all the way up to a series of waterfalls. A clear path and a relatively gentle climb, yet still offering wonderful views up into the jagged peaks of the Black Cuillins and back down to Marsco, Glamaig and Loch Sligachan. An easy way to get a taste of Skye's mountains.

Where to start

Take the road from Sligachan to Dunvegan; park in the parking area on the left hand side after a few hundred yards. (If you are approaching from Dunvegan you should go down to the hotel and turn – it is only feasible to park from that direction).

Where to go

Take the path signposted for Glenbrittle, heading up the hill beside the river (Allt Dearg) towards a white house. After five minutes the path forks and you take the slightly less well made up path to the right (there is a sign marking the way). The path, although less good from this point on, is still clear and easy enough to follow. It is a fairly gentle climb up the hill – keep going for as long as you want – with a reasonable turning point after around 20 minutes, where you reach a series of waterfalls. You can stop and sit here for a while to admire the view and the rushing water – but beware, it may be a little midgy.

Time

20 minutes to the waterfalls – you could walk for longer if you wanted (or less – the views are wonderful right from the start).

Path type

A good, clear path, but a little wet in places.

Did you know?

Sligachan is the main centre for climbers in Skye (the alternative is Glenbrittle). You will inevitably see a lot of other cars and walkers here. For many years Sligachan was the site of a major cattle market. On one occasion

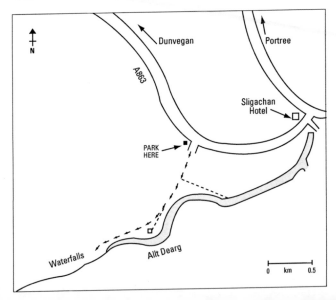

in 1794 it is reckoned there were 4,000 people and 1,600 cattle, horses and ponies at the market. When you look back down at the glen you should just about be able to picture the scene...

33 Ord

Easy walk to a lovely bay on the edge of Loch Slappin.

This is a very straightforward walk to a lovely bay in Sleat. It takes you past the house where Alexander Smith stayed when he spent his summers in Skye. Although the last time I did this I could see nothing but grey sleeting rain I am assured there are wonderful views all around here of Loch Eishort and across to the Cuillins.

Where to start

Take the road from Tarscavaig to Ord. Please note this a picturesque but quite demanding stretch of road – twisting and turning with some sharp inclines and descents – not for the faint-hearted. Park on the grassy area at the bay at Ord.

Where to go

Walk along the road slightly up the hill and turn left just after you cross the river. The road takes you past some houses and up round to the right past Ord House (where Alexander Smith stayed). The road turns into a cart track from here, taking you over the moorland. Follow this path for a good five minutes before it drops inland for a while, then back to the left and towards the sea. It eventually peters out to a grassy track but from here you can see the bay and the white house beyond it so use that as your guide. When you get near the house step over a little burn then out onto the lovely pebbly bay.

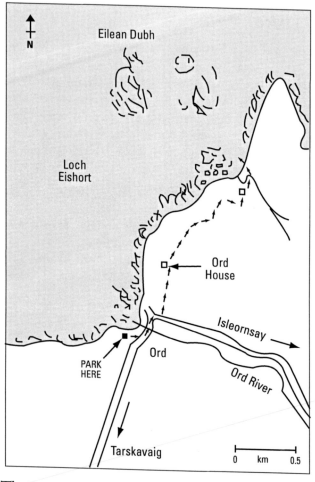

Time

22 minutes.

Path type

Minor road, cart track and grassy path (quite wet in places).

Did you know?

I will leave you with Alexander Smith's description of this area:

> 'On a fine morning there is not in the whole world a prettier sheet of water than Loch Eishort. Every thing about it is wild, beautiful and lonely. Over the Loch the Cuillins rise crested with tumult of golden mists, the shores are green behind, and away towards the horizon the Island of Rhum shoots up from the flat sea like a pointed flame.'

34 Talisker Bay

Easy walk to a gorgeous beach and picnic spot.

This is a very straightforward walk to a beautiful bay in an absolutely glorious setting. On a good day you can swim here and will certainly be tempted to paddle. Try and pick a sunny day when you can while away several hours at the shore.

Where to start

From Carbost take the turning to the left just before the distillery and then follow signs for Talisker. There are glorious views all the way down this road, first of the Cuillins then, as you approach the coast, across the sea to the Outer Isles. When you reach the farm buildings at the end of the road there is a signposted area for parking.

Where to go

Head straight towards the sea from the car park (ignoring the other paths – one to the right for Fiskavaig and the other ahead and slightly to the right for Talisker House). Your path is marked 'Talisker House Private Road No Cars' (it is fine for pedestrians and pedal cyclists though).

Follow this well made up path running beside the garden wall at Talisker House, then when the path splits at the gate take the right hand path towards the beach. This takes you through a slightly wooded area – you should be able to catch a glimpse of Talisker House to

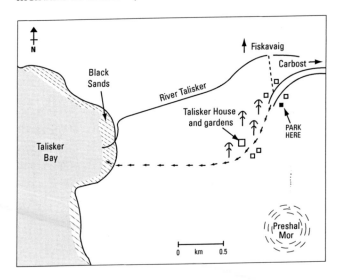

your right. There are a number of farm buildings to
your left. Keep going along this path, over a burn,
through another gate, then all the way down to the
black sands at the shore.

On the walk back enjoy the view of Preshal Mor – the
great rock that towers over the glen.

Time

25 minutes.

Path type

This is a well made up path all the way – you just need
to cross over some rocks at the end to get to the beach.

Did you know?

Talisker is Norse for 'the House of the Rock'. It lies in the shadow of *Preshal Mor* (the Great Hill), the huge rock you will see behind you as you walk down to the shore. The sand at Talisker (as on many beaches on Skye) is black. I found it quite wet to sit on even when apparently firm to the touch – you might prefer to sit on the rocks. There are excellent flat rocks to the north of the bay that are perfect for picnicking and sunbathing.

35 Kylerhea Otter Hide

Forest walk to an otter hide.

This is a well publicised Forestry Commission walk. It would be a long drive just for the sake of this short trip but it is worth doing if you're arriving or leaving by the Glenelg ferry. It's a good path to the hide, accessible to all. There's something exciting about the air of anticipation at the otter hide but you need to be patient to see anything – and the kids need to keep quiet too.

Where to start

From the Glenelg car ferry take the road up the hill, then the turning to the right. There is a signpost pointing you to the hide but it is a little hard to see. A short distance along you will reach the car park at the start of the walk (there are also toilets and an information centre a little further along).

Where to go

Follow the path – it is wide and clear, and well signposted. It splits after 10 minutes and you take the right hand fork signposted for the viewing hide. After a couple of minutes you fork again down to the hide. When you have finished at the observation point you retrace your steps to the path – from here either go left back to the car, or turn to the right. This takes you along the river side, down and then up hill again (not such a good path here), then up wooden steps and over a wooden bridge, then up again alongside the river until you rejoin the main path. If you keep going right here the path eventually opens up out of the trees, offering lovely views back over the water. You should be able to see the ferry crossing back and forth between Kylerhea and Glenelg. Once you turn back this path will take you all the way back to the car park.

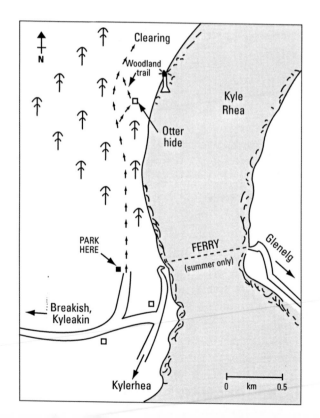

Time

25 minutes for the longer walk but only 10 minutes to the hide.

Path type

Well made up path most of the way; it is quite muddy underfoot if you take the river detour.

Did you know?

This area is maintained by the Forestry Commission. The shoreline is largely inaccessible and undisturbed, which is why it is an ideal place for otters. If you don't see any otters you are sure to see other wildlife (birds and seals for example). The longer walk described here offers wonderful views back over the straights. Although now best known as the ferry crossing, this used to be a cattle crossing – 8,000 cattle a year used to swim across the fast flowing water.

36 Loch Losait

Explore one of the most secluded bays on Skye.

This is a lovely walk taking you to a beautiful hidden bay. It is one of my favourite 'cheat' walks, picking up the tail end of a longer forest walk from one side of the Waternish peninsula to the other – you join it for the last 20 minutes or so, including the final steep descent down to the shore.

Where to start

Take the road to Stein, and then keep going ahead for Hallin. Turn right for Geary (also signposted for the school) and just after the school turn right again for Gillen. Park carefully in the turning area at the end of the road.

Where to go

Take the path that follows on from the end of the road, over a gate and along the path bearing left after a few minutes. After 10 minutes, when the path splits, take the right hand fork (going over the gate) to pick up the main path that has come from the other side of the peninsula. Follow this path along until you reach the very wide path that has been made up for Forestry Commission vehicles. Take the path that goes downhill and to the left – after a few minutes it swings back round to the right and then descends very steeply down to the bay.

To return, retrace your steps – bearing in mind that

the first part of the journey is quite a steep climb.
Keep going straight at the top of the hill (not left to
the forest). Remember to cut back off the main path
after 15 to 20 minutes – go over the gate and pick up
your original minor path to the straggle of houses at
Gillen.

Time

25 – 30 minutes.

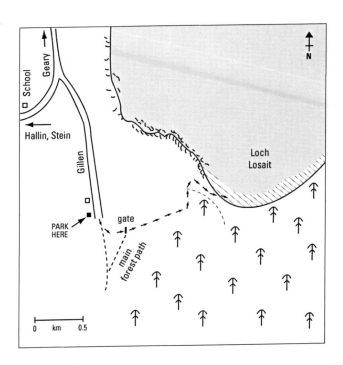

Path type

Good, clear path most of the way, and a very wide track at the end.

Did you know?

The large sea loch you are looking out to from the bay is Loch Snizort. You can just see Uig across the other side and may spot a CalMac ferry heading to the Outer Isles. The islands in the Loch are the Ascribs – seven altogether, all uninhabited.

37 Trumpan Headland

A glorious walk along the Waternish headland.

This walk offers wonderful views back to Trumpan
Church, Ardmore, Dunvegan Head and the Outer Isles.
It is a very quiet spot, with just the birds wheeling in
the wind for company. It is often quite breezy and the
walk will leave you feeling refreshed and invigorated.

Where to start

Drive north from Stein along the Waternish peninsula
and follow the signs for Trumpan. Park in the parking
area opposite the ruined church.

Where to go

From the car park turn left and walk along the road
away from the church towards a group of houses. Just
as the road turns to the right take the footpath off to
the left, signposted for Unish. (If you want a longer
walk you can follow the path all the way out to this
ruined township). Follow this path all the way (going
over/through a couple of gates at the start). After
about 25 minutes on this path you reach your turning
point – a memorial cairn on the left.

Time

33 minutes.

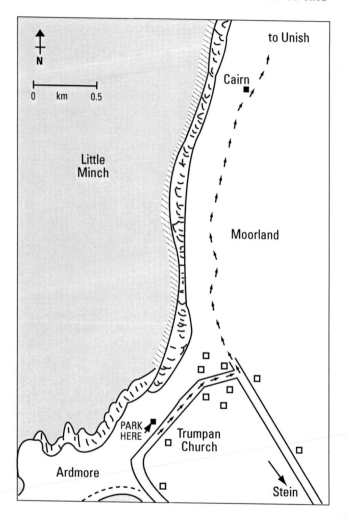

Path type

Minor road and cart track; the track is quite wet and muddy in places although you can circumnavigate most of it.

Did you know?

The memorial cairn is to Roderick MacLeod of Unish, son of John of Waternish, who fell in the second battle of Waternish. The battle was fought on this moor against the MacDonalds of Trotternish around 1530.

38 Loch Niarsco

A walk across the moor.

There is nothing particularly 'special' about this walk
but I am including it as an example of the wonderful
moorland walking that is to be found on Skye. This
walk just happened to start at the end of my road – it
took me past fields of wild flowers, through sweet
smelling moorland and banks of heather; no sound
except for birdsong and the rush of the burn; no signs
of civilisation – no houses, no cars, no buildings, no
other people in sight. Why not try this one to get the
taste of it – or look for what you can find at the end
of your own road.

Where to start

Heading from Portree to Dunvegan, take the turning
to the left for Glen Bernisdale (just after the River Tora).
Turn immediately left again behind the row of houses
and park.

Where to go

Follow the minor road past the houses gently up hill.
Go through the open gate at the end of the road and
follow the good track over the moor. Follow the path
as it veers to the right away from the trees, then
through another gate and back to the left, heading in
the direction of the wood. Go through the next gate
and you will see the burn ahead of you. About five
minutes after this the path peters out – you will see a

sheep track ahead and a grassy path to your left – take the track to the left going towards the burn – this will take you to the loch.

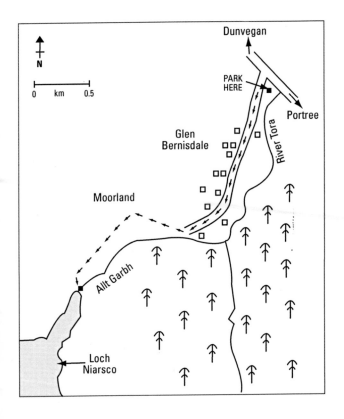

Time

33 minutes.

Path type

Minor road, cart track and grassy path – quite boggy at the end, requiring boots.

Did you know?

The walk starts in Glen Bernisdale, a place that struck me as a haven of peace of tranquillity. Things were not always so balmy however. Listen to this evidence to the Napier Commission of a man living in Glen Bernisdale in the 1880s, describing the consequences of not having the money for a horse:

'We must make a horse's work out of a woman, we get them to harrow – while slavery is done away with in other countries it is likely to continue here.'

39 Oronsay

Straightforward walk to a tidal island in Loch Bracadale.

Oronsay means Tidal Island – this walk takes you out across a causeway to the island. It is a well signed and straightforward walk (assuming you keep an eye on the tide!) offering wonderful views across to Fiskavaig and Ardtreck and the MacLeod's Maidens and Tables across the water.

Where to start

Take the minor road to Ullinish, from the Dunvegan to Sligachan road. Turn again off the loop road to get out to the point – it is signposted for Oronsay path. Park at the end of the road in the parking area.

Where to go

There is a sign pointing you to the start of the walk – to Oronsay Tidal Causeway. Go through the kissing gate and along the good track to go through a second kissing gate. Follow the path across the moor – through slightly boggy ground in places. After about 10 minutes the path peters out – bear slightly left and keep heading out for the headland. The path is pretty boggy here, but once you are over the wet ground you will reach a gateway from where you take the path down to the causeway.

The causeway itself is quite wide and long – it takes about 5 minutes to cross. You could just make this your end point – it is a lovely spot with mini-beaches where you can stop and paddle, or rocks where you can sit and admire the wonderful views.

If you keep going on the other side there is a clear path that takes you up the hill and all the way to the end of the island.

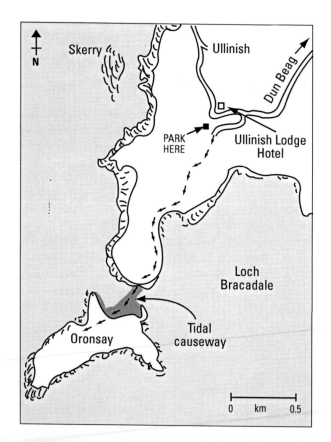

Time

35 minutes to the end of the island.

Path type

Mainly a clear path but muddy in places, with a stretch of bog that you need to cross in the middle.

Did you know?

Before rejoining the main Dunvegan/Sligachan road you might want to stop at Dun Beag Broch – you will find it at the junction with the Ullinish road. It is one of the best preserved brochs in Skye, and is looked after by Historic Scotland. In the 18thc the walls were still about 18 foot high – they are now down to about 12 foot but it is still a very impressive site.

40 Hallaig

Stunning coastal walk with poetry, cleared houses and memories.

This is both an emotional pilgrimage and a wonderful walk through some absolutely glorious scenery to a spot made famous by Sorley MacLean's poem of the same name. The walk to the memorial cairn (with an inscription of Sorley's poem in English and Gaelic) is just over 30 minutes and very straightforward. It is another 20 minutes of quite rough walking to get to the ruins of the township.

Where to start

Take the road to the east out of Inverarish going through the forest, then over open moorland. This is a wonderful drive offering tremendous views back to the Cuillins. When you get to Fearns stop at the end of the road and park just before the house.

Where to go

The track starts at the end of the road. For the first ten minutes the path is clear and flat – you could make this a very short walk in itself: the chance to enjoy the amazing views back to the Cuillins and across to the mainland should certainly not be missed.

After 10 to 15 minutes the path gets a bit wetter and more overgrown, then starts a fairly long, slow ascent. After about 35 minutes walking you will reach the memorial cairn.

If you want to keep going to Hallaig take the path through the wood – very muddy at this point – then through bracken and down a hill into another wood. You then cross the burn and go up the hill through grass and bracken to the sheep pens and what is left of the ruined township.

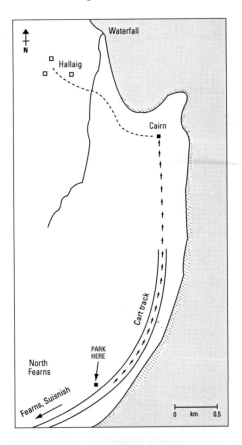

Time

35 minutes to the cairn (and another 20 minutes or so to Hallaig itself).

Path type

Initially a very good grassy path, then a narrower path which is wet and boggy in places (you would need boots). After the cairn the path is rough and very wet and muddy.

Did you know?

The Napier Commission in the 1880s provided the opportunity for the crofters to describe their experiences of the clearances that had taken place 30 or more years before. Donald MacLeod, giving evidence to the Commission in Torran, at the north end of Raasay, described the earlier evictions from Hallaig and the other townships on the island:

'The townships were altogether arable land capable of being ploughed. Now they are all in the proprietor's hands and the only inhabitants of the land today are rabbits and deer and sheep.'

He also described the pain of the people being cleared from their homeland:

'They were weeping and wailing and lamenting, taking handfuls of grass that was growing over the graves of their families in the churchyard, as remembrances of their kindred.'

The cairn at the end of this walk is dedicated to the people of Hallaig and the other crofting townships.

Further Reading

TWO COMPANION GUIDES to Skye have been highlighted in this book. One is Otta Swire's *Skye: The Island and its Legends*. First published in the 1950s the book captures many of the old stories and legends about the island. It can be a little hard to get hold of, but you may see copies when you are on the island. Published by Maclean Press (1999), ISBN 1899272070

Alexander Smith wrote his famous prose poem *A Summer in Skye* in 1864. It is a vivid description of six happy weeks he spent on the island, capturing the history, culture and mood of the times. He also manages to convey both the spirit of the place and the emotions it can stir in the visitor. It is an enjoyable read and good to dip into when you are on the island. Published by Birlinn (2004), ISBN 1874744386

Derek Cooper's gazetteer *Skye* is a useful introduction to the places, culture and history of the island. Published by Birlinn (1995), ISBN 1874744378.

If you are interested in the troubled history of the 19thc on Skye, from the Clearances to the Crofters' War, A D Cameron's *Go Listen to the Crofters* is an excellent place to start. The book pulls together evidence given to the Napier Commission in 1883, including much interesting testimony from Skye and Raasay. Published by Acair (1997), ISBN 0861520637

Skye Place Names

PLACE NAMES IN SKYE reflect both Gaelic and Norse influence. Some of the more common words you will find on the island are given below.

Gaelic

Abhainn	river
Allt	burn
Ard	high point
Ban	fair
Beag	small
Beinn	mountain
Camas	bay
Caol (kyle)	narrow stretch of water
Ceann (ken, kin)	head
Cill (kil)	church
Coire	circular hollow, corry
Dearg	red
Dubh	dark, black
Eilean	island
Mor	great, large
Taigh	house

Norse

Ay (ey)	island (e.g. Soay, Pabbay)
Bost	farmhouse, dwelling
Ness (nish)	point, headland
Vik (vaig)	creek or bay

Easy Walks in Badenoch and Strathspey: Monarch of the Glen Country

Ernest Cross

ISBN 1 84282 093 1 PBK £4.99

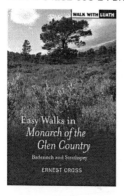

Based on its predecessor, *Short Walks in the Cairngorms*, this book is a clear and comprehensive guide to a selection of easygoing yet scenic walks in the areas of Scottish countryside made popular by the BBC television series *Monarch of the Glen*.

Perfect for novice and amateur walkers as well as families, *Easy Walks in Monarch of the Glen Country: Badenoch and Strathspey* is a lively pocket companion that provides a wealth of information to the reader, including detailed route plans of each walk, invaluable safety tips, basic hillwalking instruction and practical local advice. A comprehensive guide to the wildlife, history and surroundings of the area helps to make the scenic Cairngorms landscape come alive.

On the hills or at home by the fire, *Easy Walks in Monarch of the Glen Country: Badenoch and Strathspey* makes inspiring and essential reading for anyone interested in walking in the Cairngorm area.